# Woodpeckers

# GEORGE K. PECK

SMART APPLE MEDIA

Published by

Smart Apple Media

123 South Broad Street

Mankato, Minnesota  56001

☙

Copyright © 1998 Smart Apple Media.

Photos by George K. Peck,

James Richards,

Mark Peck,

Bill Brockett / UNIPHOTO

Editorial assistance by Barbara Ciletti

**Library of Congress Cataloging-in-Publication Data**

Peck, George K.

Woodpeckers / written by George Peck.

p.  cm.

Includes index.

Summary: Describes the physical characteristics, behaviors, and habitats

of various species of woodpeckers.

ISBN 1-887068-12-0

1.  Woodpeckers—Juvenile literature.  [1.  Woodpeckers.]  I.  Title.

QL696.P56P435   1998                              96-18154

598.7'2—dc20                                      CIP

                                                  AC

5  4  3  2

# CONTENTS

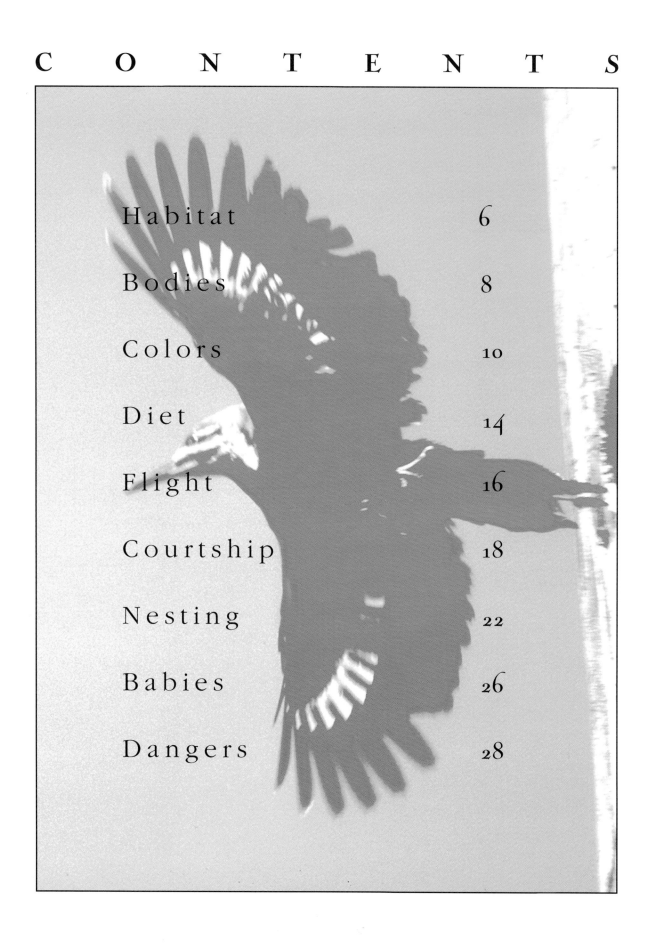

The forest
is

never silent.

A distant honking could be traffic on a faraway freeway, or a flock of wild Canada geese. That scraping, gnawing sound could be a porcupine chewing bark, two branches rubbing together, or a proud stag polishing his antlers. The rustling noise could be a mouse foraging for seeds, a fox stalking a partridge, or only the wind on fallen leaves.

**But one sound is distinctive.**

When you hear a rapid hammering sound, faster than any human drummer, echoing through the trees, you've heard a woodpecker.

There are 214 species of woodpeckers in the world. Nearly everywhere trees grow, woodpeckers thrive. Only Australia, Madagascar, New Guinea, and some other smaller islands do not have woodpeckers.

In the United States and Canada, we have 21 different types of woodpeckers. From the evergreen forests of Canada to Florida's Everglades, from the towering redwoods of the northwest coast to the cactus-covered deserts of the southwest, the sound of their hammering fills the air.

Woodpeckers must have wood to peck, so most North American woodpeckers live in wooded areas. They are common in both evergreen forests and in leafy deciduous woodlands.

In tall pine and fir forests of the western United States and Canada lives the White-headed Woodpecker. The Three-toed Woodpecker is found in the spruce forests of the far north. The Black-backed Woodpecker also lives in the far north, but prefers areas that have been burned in forest fires, with many dead trees. The Red-breasted Sapsucker lives along the western coast of the United States and the pine and aspen woods of Canada.

Many other species, such as the Red-naped Sapsucker and Nuttall's Woodpecker, are found in broad-leafed or deciduous woodlands. The Acorn Woodpecker lives in oak forests where there is a good supply of acorns.

Northern Flickers, one of our most common woodpeckers, are found all over North America in gardens and parks. The Downy and Hairy Woodpeckers inhabit urban areas and are often seen on bird feeders.

The Pileated Woodpecker, the largest North American species, is found all across southern Canada and the United States, as far south as the Gulf Coast in the east and northern California in the west.

Two woodpecker species are found in the deserts of the southwest, where there are few trees. Gila and Ladder-backed Woodpeckers live in open desert areas. Instead of trees, they rely on tall cactus plants for food and shelter.

*Three-toed Woodpecker building nest.*

Woodpeckers come in many sizes. The Pileated Woodpecker is now the biggest woodpecker in North America, but that wasn't always true. The Imperial Woodpecker of Mexico, which recently became extinct, was 24 inches (60 cm) long—almost as big as a small goose! The common Downy Woodpecker is only about 6 3/4 inches (17 cm) long. The tiniest woodpecker of all is the Brown-capped Woodpecker of India and Malaysia, which is only as long as a ballpoint pen.

Because woodpeckers peck wood, they all have strong, sharp beaks. Because they cling to the sides of trees, they have short legs and strong feet with sharp, curved claws. Some woodpecker species have three toes and some have four. Two of the toes point forward and the other toe or toes point backward.

Woodpecker tails have two stiff, strong central feathers. The bird uses its tail as a prop when climbing or resting on the trunk of a tree. If you watch a woodpecker at work, you can see how it uses its claws and its stiff tail feathers to move easily up and down tree trunks.

The most remarkable thing about the woodpecker is its ability to peck wood. When a woodpecker pecks, it isn't just a peck here and another peck there. The woodpecker goes all out, pecking so hard and fast that its head becomes a blur. Wood chips fly every which way. It almost looks like the woodpecker is trying to hurt itself!

Of course, the woodpecker is perfectly happy banging its beak into tree trunks. It has a thick skull, a small, well-protected brain, and shock-absorbing muscles at the base of its beak. Its powerful neck muscles drive its head back and forth like a feathered jackhammer. It also has bristles lining its nostrils to filter out dust and tiny wood chips. Pecking wood is what the woodpecker does best.

Most woodpeckers are covered with black and white, or dark brown, feathers. The males of all North American species have a colorful red or yellow patch somewhere on their heads. Female woodpeckers are less showy, with more brown or gray in their plumage and less colorful heads.

The Pileated Woodpecker is one of the easiest woodpeckers to identify. This large black bird has a bright red pointed crest on its head and white patches on the underside of its wings.

The Red-headed Woodpecker is also easy to identify—it is the only one with a solid red head.

Downy and Hairy Woodpeckers are hard to tell apart until you see them together. The Hairy Woodpecker is much larger and has a longer beak.

The Black-backed and Three-toed Woodpeckers also look very similar. Both have three toes and a yellow patch on the males' heads, but the Black-backed Woodpecker has a solid black back, whereas the Three-toed Woodpecker has black and white bars down its back.

The Lewis Woodpecker has greenish black feathers on its head and neck, and a dark red face. The four species of sapsuckers all have pale yellow bellies, but the Red-cockaded Woodpecker is almost entirely black and white— only the tiniest tuft of red shows on the side of the male's head.

The Northern Flicker is covered in many colors, which vary from one region to another. Flickers are brown with black spots and bars, a whitish rump, a spotted belly, a gray or tan-colored face, and

a splash of red somewhere on the male's head.  In the

west, the bottoms of the flicker's wings tend to be

golden or pinkish, and the face

has a splash of red.  In the

east, the wings have a yellow

underside and the red splash is on

the back of the male's head.

Why do woodpeckers peck?

They peck to make holes to nest in. They peck to communicate with other woodpeckers. And they peck because they are hungry. A feeding woodpecker climbs up, down, and around the trunks of dead and decaying trees, listening carefully. When it hears the faint sounds of insects in their tunnels, the woodpecker hammers a hole with its sharp bill. It uses its tongue to probe for beetles and insect larvae.

The woodpecker's tongue is an insect's worst nightmare. It is sticky, has a barbed tip, and can reach deep into the insect's tunnels.

Sapsuckers get their name because they drill holes into living bark, letting the sap drip down the tree trunk. Insects come to feed on the sweet sap. The sapsucker eats both the sap and the insects. You can tell when a sapsucker has been feeding on a tree because it drills neat, regular rows of holes, leaving the trunk looking like a pegboard! Sapsuckers sometimes drill so many holes that a small tree might not survive.

Some woodpeckers feed on seeds, nuts, and berries. The Acorn Woodpecker drills holes in trees and fills the holes with acorns for its winter food supply. Acorn Woodpeckers live in colonies, or groups, of three to ten birds. Since they do everything as a group, they store enough acorns to last them for several months during the late fall and winter. One sycamore tree in California was found with 20,000 acorns stuck in its trunk!

Woodpeckers fly in a swooping, undulating motion.  They flap their wings and rise into the air, then glide down toward earth for a moment or two.  Then it's up to the sky and down again, like a boat riding the waves.  Woodpeckers usually do not fly long distances.  They prefer to flit from tree to tree.

Migration is the trip that most birds make in the spring and in the fall. Birds that feed on flowers, green plants, flying insects, or fish must fly south in the winter or they will starve.

Because insects live under the bark and in the wood of trees all year round, most woodpeckers have a steady supply of food.  They do not have to migrate.

One exception is the Yellow-bellied Sapsucker.  Sapsuckers must have running sap to eat.  Sapsuckers breed in the north during the spring and summer, but in the winter, when the sap freezes, they migrate south to Mexico and the southeastern United States.

*Yellow-bellied Sapsucker at nest site.*

During the winter, woodpeckers like to be by themselves. When spring arrives, they become more interested in other woodpeckers—especially ones of the opposite sex.

During courtship, woodpeckers call to one another with whinnying or rattle-like cries. The mating call of the Northern Flicker sounds like hiccups.

Woodpeckers also use their pecking ability to communicate with others of their species. They hammer on hollow trees, utility poles, metal roofs, or anything that will make a loud drumming sound—the louder the better. These woodpeckers aren't looking for food. They are looking for another woodpecker!

Different woodpecker species drum at different speeds and intervals. When a Downy Woodpecker hears another Downy Woodpecker drumming, it recognizes the rhythm of its own species.

Woodpeckers use drumming to attract mates, but they also use it to warn other woodpeckers away from their territory. Once a male and female wood-pecker form a pair bond, they defend their nesting area from all intruders.

Every spring, the male woodpecker chooses a tree and starts hammering away. Sometimes the female helps with the drilling. If the tree is dead and the wood is soft, it might take only a week for the woodpecker to hammer a hole big enough for a nest. If the tree is alive, the hammering could go on for months!

Flickers, Downy Woodpeckers, and Red-bellied Woodpeckers drill their nests in dead trees. Pileated Woodpeckers and Yellow-bellied Sapsuckers prefer living trees. The Red-cockaded Woodpecker nests in living pines that have a soft, diseased center. Red-headed Woodpeckers sometimes drill new nests, but usually make do with existing holes in trees, buildings, or poles.

Woodpecker cavities, or holes, measure from 6 to 18 inches (15 to 46 cm) deep, forming a dark tunnel or cave. They are wider at the bottom where the eggs sit. Once drilling is complete, the male moves the wood chips on the floor and makes a mat that will cushion the eggs and keep them all in one place. The new home is ready.

After mating, the female usually lays a clutch, or group, of three to five eggs, but not at the same time. She'll lay one egg every day until her clutch is complete. All woodpeckers lay white eggs. Most birds that nest in dark cavities lay white eggs. Because the eggs are well-hidden, they do not need the camouflage of dark colors and speckles, and the white eggs are easier to see in the dark.

Both the male and the female sit on the eggs to keep them warm. This is called incubation. In most species, the male incubates the eggs at night, and the female incubates during the day. The heat from their bodies helps the embryos grow inside the eggs. Incubation usually takes about two weeks.

Baby woodpeckers come into the world blind, naked, and small enough to sit in a soup spoon. They are just as helpless as you were on the day you were born. Their parents take turns leaving the nest to search for insects.

The mother and father swallow insects and store them in their crops. Crops are special food storage sacks at the wide part of a bird's throat. A mother woodpecker swallows food until her crop is full. Then she returns to her nest and brings up food from her crop and gives it to the babies.

Baby woodpeckers grow very rapidly. They may eat as often as every 15 minutes. Their mother and father stay busy getting food until their youngsters can find it for themselves.

When they are ten days old, the babies' eyes are open. They hiss and cry, especially when they hear their mother or father return to the nest with something to eat. Small feathers grow in patches, and in three weeks, they're ready to climb up the wall of their home and sit at the entrance to the nest. Their parents get quite a greeting when they return!

After four weeks, or about a month, the babies aren't babies anymore. They have grown into fledglings, which means that they have nearly all of their feathers. It's time to explore the world. The fledglings perch at the entrance to the nest and flap their wings until they're in the air.

The fledglings quickly learn to drill for food. Ant hills, dead trees, and live trees become schools for survival. The young woodpeckers may follow their parents for several weeks, begging for food, but soon they learn to find their own meals.

As soon as the young woodpeckers are on their own, the parents might raise a second brood in the same nest cavity, or they might start all over again, drilling a new nest hole.

Like all birds, the woodpecker leads a dangerous life. Hawks and owls take both young and adult woodpeckers. Squirrels and tree-climbing snakes might raid nests, stealing eggs before they hatch. Other birds, such as the European Starling, sometimes take over a woodpecker's nesting cavity before it has a chance to lay its eggs. In the northeastern United States, starlings have taken over many of the nesting sites used by Red-headed Woodpeckers. This once-common woodpecker species is now a rare sight in that part of the country.

The Red-cockaded Woodpecker has a special way of protecting its nest. This bird drills its nest cavity in living pine trees, causing sap to ooze out of the tree and around the nest hole. The sticky sap is irritating to snakes and may also discourage other predators.

Some woodpecker species are threatened by loss of habitat. Pileated Woodpeckers usually live on large tracts of old forest. When Europeans first arrived on the shores of America, they found a land covered with dense forests. During the 1700s and on into the early 1800s, trees were leveled to build homes and make room for farming.

The Pileated Woodpeckers fled to more remote areas as the forests were cleared. They had fewer and fewer places to live. Their larger relative, the Ivory-billed Woodpecker, disappeared completely and has not been seen since the 1950s.

Fortunately, many of our old forests are being preserved, and the Pileated Woodpecker has learned to adapt to younger forests and to human development.

With their red caps and distinctive hammering, woodpeckers are one of our most interesting and popular bird families. Like all creatures, woodpeckers play an important role in the forest ecosystem. They help control insect populations, and they provide shelter for other animals by drilling new tree cavities every spring.

Bird species such as Eastern Bluebirds and Wood Ducks use old woodpecker holes for their own nesting sites. Many tree-dwelling mammals, including squirrels and Pine Martens, also make their homes in holes originally drilled by woodpeckers.

The Yellow-bellied Sapsucker, by killing small trees with its drilling, helps thin out overcrowded stands of trees. It also provides food for hummingbirds in the early spring, before the wildflowers bloom. The hummingbirds feed on the sweet sap!

As long as our woodlands and forests are preserved, the drumming of woodpeckers will echo through the trees.

# I N D E X